THE GAME & FISH MASTERY LIBRARY

PHEASANT & QUAIL

THE GAME & FISH MASTERY LIBRARY

PHEASANT & QUAIL

By S.G.B. Tennant, Jr.
Photography by Arie de Zanger

WILLOW CREEK PRESS

Minocqua, Wisconsin

Published by Willow Creek Press
P.O. Box 147
Minocqua, Wisconsin 54548

Designed by Heather M. McElwain

For information on other Willow Creek titles, call 1-800-850-9453

Library of Congress Cataloging-in-Publication Data
ISBN 1-57223-181-5

Printed in Canada

TABLE OF CONTENTS

FOREWORD

In the very old days I was a young apprentice at the Hotel Pierre in New York. The world was rich and jazzy then, but even at that time haute cuisine and the cooking of wild game were not often associated in this country. Eventually game farms on Long Island began to produce beautiful pheasant and quail that found their way onto the menus of André Soltner, Henri Soulé, Pierre Franey and other great cuisiniers.

Amidst this explosion of culinary interest in America I became Chef at the New York Racquet and Tennis Club, as it is now known, where I presided for over thirty years. During that time a legion of young New Yorkers and sports men and women from all over the world came through our tables on Park Avenue. For many it was the first realization of the charm of pheasant and quail as haute cuisine.

I enjoyed preparing hundreds of banquets and private meals using classical presentations such as those found here. In those days the club members often brought their own shot game and the affairs were like a family cookout with me at the grill. In today's world, however, the farm-raised birds are far more uniform and reliable for the sophisticated applications.

Pheasant & Quail is an engaging collection of traditional approaches to game birds. The mysteries are explained; the results are accessible. This is a "cross-over" book that blends the very best of classical cooking with the practical realities of the modern home kitchen.

I hope that home gourmets and professional chefs will appreciate the experience distilled into these lovely presentations.

Bon Appetit!

— *Chef Felix Antonecchia, retired*
Chef de Cuisine, New York Racquet and Tennis Club

INTRODUCTION

When this all started thirty-five years ago I was the junior cornbread cook at our offshore island duck camp. My father, Borden Tennant, was the club president and cook. The mission was to eat as well as possible in our constrained circumstances.

Horseradish was hard to come by. Lettuce had to be brought down by boat from the mainland. But there were good times aplenty, and no scarcity of ducks and oysters and redfish, which we gathered up by the skiffload. Those were the best of times, and they proved for me the bond between good eating and good company.

My father was at the time a member of a fledgling chapter of "Les Amis d' Escoffier" and with his *Guide Culinaire* tucked under his arm we produced everything from oyster soufflé to red heads bigarade for the joy and amusement of our hunting pals. That was my foundation. And since then I have learned from chefs, great and small, and I have learned from ancient tomes. But the best learning, I believe, is in doing.

The only real credentials I bring to this enterprise are a lifetime of game cooking all over the world, and an enthusiasm for more informed cooking and the good times it engenders. Those good times have brought me into the company of some pretty fine chefs, and some pretty fine people. As a way of life, I can heartily attest that game cooking is good for the soul.

For years I had the honor of acting as food editor for several outdoor magazines, and the people I encountered were invariably first-class sportsmen. One of the most rewarding encounters was with famous photographer Arie de Zanger, who very kindly agreed to "shoot" this book.

Arie has done fish and game and wine photography all over the world. His work on any number of books is groundbreaking. We have had some hilarious times together, and being able to rely on his experience and judgment over the last fifteen years has been a great resource for me.

And the really good news is Wilma de Zanger, his talented, thoughtful and creative wife, who was the food stylist for this book. Wilma is a steady voice to talk with, and she has understood and mastered every culinary procedure that the world of haute cuisine has thrown at her, and added something in the bargain.

I hope this book will bring home gourmets into closer contact with the joys of pheasant and quail. These birds are no longer the exclusive preserve of the sporting enthusiasts, or the aristocrat, and in an era where thoughtful dining is now fashionable again let us pick up the challenge of game birds. The rewards are of historic proportions.

Acknowledgments are a big part of bringing a cookbook together. The credits go up and down the ladder from the practical use of a platter in a photograph, to the philosophical nudges about sauces and seasonings.

Arie asked me to specially mention the folks at Rosenthal, Ltd. in New York, particularly Dorlise O'Hara for the use of some exquisite porcelain, and also Desiree Shaughnessy for propping many of the still lifes.

The proof of the timeliness of this book is the fact that we here, and the folks in the studios, all got our birds over the phone. Whether from D'Artagnan, Inc.; Manchester Quail Farms; Polarica, Inc.; Lobels; or Czimer's — America's game birds are ready for the asking.

Cooking pheasant and quail is reserved for people who have fun in life, people who can make choices about how they live and what they love. And so it is with a deep breath of gratitude that I thank my very splendid partner and wife Jane for her thoughtful, provocative assistance in the kitchen and in life. Allow me to dedicate this effort to her as she has made it all such great fun.

Let me know what you think. Good cooking.

— *S.G.B. Tennant, Jr.*
Helena, Texas

PHEASANT

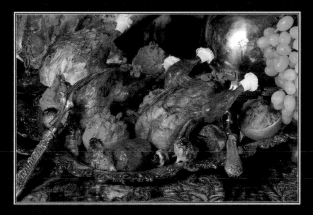

"A MOST EXCELLENT BIRD"
— Edward, Prince of Wales

In England they once made a spectacle of shooting pheasant. Squads of beaters pushed, herded, and cajoled the birds into flying over a line of heavily armed guests. It was a great social event, with a gallery of observers standing a few paces back, rather an early sporting clays, with live targets.

Some of the best shots were ladies, unimpeded by their ankle-length dresses and bustles. Lord Ripon, however, always took home the first prize in the shooting department, and on one notorious Saturday a hundred years ago he shot 28 pheasant inside a minute's time.

At lunch time the keeper blew a whistle and the beaters retired to the barn for a lunch of pork pie and cider. Prince Edward and his thirty guests, on the other hand, sat down to a banquet: champagne was poured out and Edward, Prince of Wales, toasted the pheasant, ". . . a most excellent bird."

The Edwardian Era witnessed a rise in culinary interest, with the pheasant at its center. Ambitious chefs from Escoffier onward celebrated the pheasant as terrine, galantine, salmis, parfait, and beyond; but always with a tip of their toque to the sauce.

And without great sauces, the pheasant is something less. Dark reduction sauces, relying heavily on a veal stock, a touch of wine, and a contrasting fruit flavor are the lessons of the masters. By careful attention to these details one produces a reduction that becomes an echo that re-sounds the delicate note of flavor initiated by the bird itself, and which is expressed again in the bouquet and finally the sauce.

One of the earliest great sauces was The Prince of Wales Sauce that graced the roast pheasant. It was a rich reduction of orange juice, port wine, and the drippings from the roast pan, topped with a glass of champagne.

Many great chefs developed sauces with colorful names — Diana, Poivrade, Bigarade and more — and eventually these were brought to America by the great missionary chefs, such as Henri Soulé at the restaurant Le Pavillion in New York.

Soulé was very much old school, and kept his secrets in reserve. As a matter of principle he would never have catered off premises or sent a terrine down to a private picnic, except in an emergency.

I remember one such emergency, however, and it was on the eve of the National Retriever Championships in 1961. John Olin, titan of industry, Commander-in-Chief of Winchester-Western, etc., had five dogs entered, but nothing to serve his guests at the tailgate lunch that went hand in hand with the retriever trial.

One evening at the restaurant Olin explained to the great chef about retriever trials, and the social ambiance, and how much he needed a pheasant terrine "to go." It is not clear how much of this the mostly French-speaking chef took in, but Soulé finally agreed to send along a trio of specially prepared pheasant terrines.

As they packed the terrines in wicker hampers in the back of Olin's Rolls Royce outside the old Le Pavillion on Fifty-fifth Street in Manhattan, Soulé patted his benefactor on the shoulder, "Even if your dogs do not catch the rabbit, you will have my little pheasants to eat! N'est ce pas?"

Those were glamorous terrines, calculated to gobsmock the gentry, and a long shot from what usually happens to a pheasant taken by the typical party of three men and a dog trudging through the frozen corn stubble of a contemporary Kansas winter. Nevertheless, pheasant as food also has a sturdy bourgeois appeal. The Cacciatore, or "hunter" recipe used here is from the Italian mountians, and in a pinch can be cooked over an open fire without pots or pans.

Today's farm-raised birds are in every way superior to the birds the old chefs raved about, but the secret of the old timers' success, their masterful sauces, is as important today as ever, and as available to any cook willing to turn a hand in the kitchen.

All rich sauces, bar none, have a great stock at their heart, and the richer the sauce, the more likely that it is based on a veal stock. I hasten to add that there are, of course, perfectly acceptable sauces made with tomato paste and flour, but they never achieve the color, texture, or layered depth of flavors that a reduction of veal stock can provide. It is worth the effort, and the difference is evident.

One novel combination of sauces and flavors came from Alfred DeGuoy, "gros bonnet" at the Glean Eagles Hotel in Scotland for many years before the war. He recognized the affinity of pheasant to Marsala, and later Madeira, when combined with juniper berry.

In the old days at Glen Eagles they served fried hominy with the braised birds, and the bright, almost crunchy corn picked up and enhanced the orange sweetness of the sauce. DeGuoy's magic was the introduction of the exotic fennel and juniper berry to send the flavors off the scale.

Every hunt I have visited presents the old problem of "hanging pheasant" in new ways. On the one hand are the upholders of the old European traditions, blessed with cold, dry climates who insist on a seven day "mortification" of the whole bird. On the other hand you have the bright, modern and enlightened group, naturally including myself, who suggest a limited, modified hangout in the refrigerator for a few days.

I remember sitting in a little tavern in the wild pheasant country of South Dakota one breezy October evening a number of years ago. The bar was called "The Ringneck" and I was in the company of two senior pheasant hunters, Homer Circle and Zack Taylor. We had spent the afternoon prowling the fields for pheasant, exploring the small brakes and grass valleys with my old Labrador retriever Gabriella.

By lunch we needed one more bird, and as we walked back to the car to change locations, up it burst, hanging overhead, it seemed, for almost an hour. One shot. Two. Then a rattling fusillade that sounded like seven more, and the bird fell neatly between us.

My old Labrador sat spellbound throughout this performance. Her eyes bulged larger with each shot. Zack claimed that he waited until the two of us were empty, and that it was, in fact, his first shot that collected the bird and closed the matter. Amid great shouts of incredulity we went back to The Ringneck, and tried to work out our evening menu.

I suggested fresh mushrooms from the Dakota prairie. Zack howled. "Hunger makes the best sauce," he said, quoting an old Canadian moose guide.

Homer wagged his finger at me, "You have written somewhere that these birds must be hung! So let us consider . . . The parking lot? The hotel lobby? Where shall we hang these birds to discover their essence?"

We marched into the kitchen, and the astonished cook took inspiration from our enthusiasm.

"Give me an hour," he said, "and I'll do a poacher's pot pie with a pastry lid that'll taste as good as Christmas goose."

It was much later that evening when we worked our way through our puff pastry crusted pot pies. All was right with the world, and even Homer seemed pleased.

"Let me point out," he said in his professorial voice, "This is a most excellent bird. And the only hanging it did was in the air over Zack Taylor's head."

Zack thundered back in his Northwoods French patois, "After all, mon amis, it is now nearly midnight. And is it not true, 'Hunger always makes the best sauce!'"

Cold Buffet of Pheasant Ballotine

The illustrious Fernand Point once circulated a Christmas card showing the Sunday buffet in the gardens of his restaurant La Pyramide, on a sunny day in Vienne, France. Point stood proudly beside a trellis of small flowers and offered a cold ballotine of pheasant. The old maestro had grown to three stars under the "ancien regime," and his pheasant ballotine was worth more than a detour, it was the destination.

2 pheasant, whole, double breasted for ballotine
½ cup cooked smoked ham, cut in cubes
1½ cups stale corn bread, for stuffing
2 tablespoons chopped parsley

1 egg, slightly beaten
Salt and pepper
4 tablespoons melted butter

Each ballotine is made from the entire pheasant skin of one bird with meat attached, and bones discarded. (*See page 74 for illustration of the boning and rolling technique.*)

After boning the pheasant, lay the resulting skin and meat combination on the counter, skin down, meat up, revealing the trench between the two breasts intended to receive meat pared from the leg bones, and eventually the stuffing. Do not worry about slight tears in the skin.

To make the stuffing, the smoked ham should be placed in a processor with the cornbread, parsley, egg, half of the melted butter, and salt and pepper. Whirl for a few seconds to mix thoroughly, and reduce the meat size to tiny points. Spread half of the mixture evenly over each of the two pheasant skins.

Form the rolls from the head toward the tail, lifting the skin at the head and rolling it over the stuffing and continue rolling until the tail skin has wrapped into place. Close the roll with four small poultry skewers, and wrap with cotton string and place in a shallow roasting pan before going on to the next roll.

Preheat the oven to 350°F. Bake the ballotines in the remaining melted butter for one hour, turning three times and basting three times, adding oil as needed to avoid burning. Remove the rolls from the oven and cool. Remove the skewers and string and cut in transverse ½-inch slices, sausagelike. Arrange on a cold buffet with green beans vinaigrette and a tossed cabbage salad.

ROAST PHEASANT WITH PRINCE OF WALES SAUCE

Select only young birds for roasting, and take pains to protect the bird against drying out in the hot oven.
This is done by larding in one form or another, and the use of caul is highly recommended because of the flavor and the color that it brings.
The use of thyme-seasoned butter also protects the birds' moistness when it is recirculated through basting.
Decorate the pheasant drumsticks with paper frills and serve with parsley and roast potatoes.

Brace of pheasant, 2 birds, picked and oven-ready
4 ounces thyme-seasoned butter
2 sheets pork caul (omental fat), or 4 slices uncooked
 bacon
Salt and pepper
2 cups mushrooms

½ cup flour, seasoned with salt and pepper
1 cup veal stock
2 cups port wine
2 tablespoons butter
1 glass of champagne

Thyme Butter Cream: To 4 ounces of butter at room temperature, add 1 teaspoon ground thyme and 4 anchovy filets (patted dry) and blend with a fork.

Prince of Wales Sauce: Remove the fat from the pan juices, then add 2 tablespoons butter, and 1 generous wine glass of champagne, and bring to a boil on the top of the stove, stirring from the bottom of the pan, and reduce to nearly nothing. Then add 2 cups of port wine or optional Port Wine Sauce (*recipe on page 83*). Heat to the boiling point and reduce slightly to a glaze with which to coat the birds upon serving with red currant jelly.

Spread half of the thyme butter across the skin of each bird. Salt and pepper the inside and outside of the bird lightly. Apply the pork caul by wrapping it gently around each bird once and securing it to a leg or wing. Trim any excess and tuck it inside the bird.

Prepare a roasting pan with rack, and 1 cup of veal stock below to prevent scorching. Place the birds breast down to begin, and introduce them in a hot, preheated oven, 425°F. After 20 minutes turn the birds over and spread the remaining thyme butter over the breasts and continue roasting at 375°F for another 20 minutes. Baste once or twice if the bird is browning too quickly. Pheasants generally require 20 minutes per pound plus 10 minutes. (*Recipe continued on page 22.*)

Roast Pheasant with Prince of Wales Sauce (continued)

After 40 minutes, remove the birds and dust the breasts lightly with the seasoned flour over the caul, and return, breasts up, to the oven for 10 minutes or until browned, without basting. If you have used bacon or pork fat back to lard the birds, it should be removed before dusting the birds with the flour. Remove the birds and keep them warm on a platter while the sauce is prepared.

Cossack Pheasant with Blini

Serve this venerable dish with little pancakes of Blini made from whole-grain flour, yeast, and eggs, and fried in butter.

1 pheasant, cut into 8 serving pieces
6 tablespoons butter
2 tablespoons lard
½ cup vodka

1 cup onions, finely diced
½ cup white wine
1 cup sour cream
Salt and pepper

Season the pheasant pieces with salt and pepper and sauté in the butter and lard until slightly underdone, about 20 minutes. Remove the pheasant from the pan.

To the hot juices in the pan add the vodka, and over low heat scrape and stir to deglaze the pan. Add the onions and continue stirring over low heat until they are softened but not browned. Add the wine and continue over low heat until reduced by half. Add the sour cream, and simmer for 5 minutes until blended. Return the pheasant pieces to the sauce and warm gently.

PHEASANT TERRINE Á LA BELLE ÉPOQUE

This elaborate presentation during the Belle Époque of French cuisine, and for many years thereafter, was the private preserve of the great professional chefs. The magic of terrine construction and composition was shrouded in secrecy, and the techniques were jealously guarded. Not everyone knew how, or even cared to make the attempt. Eventually, of course, the great chefs spread out around the globe, taking their wisdom with them.

2 pheasant
⅓ cup olive oil
I carrot, sliced
I large onion, sliced
Bouquet garni and bay leaf
I dried red pepper
I teaspoon salt
2 quats water
I clove garlic, peeled
I clove garlic, crushed
12 juniper berries
2 shallots
2 tablespoons butter

2 tablespoons brandy
8 white peppercorns, crushed
4 slices unsmoked bacon
I½ teaspoons pâté salt (*recipe on page 88*)
I tablespoon orange rind, grated
I clove garlic, minced
⅓ cup brandy
2 eggs
½ cup chicken livers (or foie gras) marinated in brandy
I teaspoon salt
White pepper and salt to taste
½ cup chopped almonds or pistachio nuts
Port wine aspic to cover (*recipe on page 84*)

Bone the birds, discarding skin, tendon and fat. Reserve 3 cups of meat, and refrigerate. With kitchen mallet and shears break and shear the bones and carcass, rub with olive oil, and roast in 350°F oven for 30 minutes, turning 3 times to assure an even browning on the bones.

Combine the bones, carcass, carrot, onion, bouquet garni, peeled garlic clove, red pepper, juniper berries and water in a large pot and simmer for one hour to make a game broth or "fumet." Strain the bones and vegetables and return the broth to the pot and set on the fire. Increase heat and reduce to 2 cups. (*Recipe continued on page 26.*)

PHEASANT TERRINE Á LA BELLE ÉPOQUE (CONTINUED)

In a sauté pan soften the shallots in butter without browning. Strain the reduced game broth, add half of the citrus rind, scraping and shaking the pan. Over moderate heat, reduce this combination to a syrupy essence, about half a cup, being careful not to scorch. Cool and reserve.

Keep all meat, fat and bowls chilled to ensure maximum blending. Cut the reserved and chilled pheasant meat into large pieces, add the remaining citrus rind, and crushed garlic. Chill.

Chop the chilled fatback alone with the cutter blade of a food processor for 1 full minute. With the processor off add the ⅓ cup brandy, eggs, pâté salt and chicken livers and continue processing until the mixture is liquefied. Add the 3 cups of pheasant meat and continue processing briefly, less than 30 seconds, being careful to preserve identifiable pheasant meat size. In a large mixing bowl combine the meat mixture, the 2 cups of reduced essence, the nuts, and the crushed white peppercorns evenly into the forcemeat.

Butter the sides and bottom of a one-quart terrine. Carefully pack the forcemeat into the terrine, avoiding air pockets. Do not fill beyond the lower lip of the terrine.

Butter the underside of a sheet of aluminum foil and lay across the forcemeat, crimping the edges lightly. Place the lid of the terrine over the foil, and bake in a bain marie, in the oven preheated to 350°F with preheated water (hot tap 130°F). Carefully regulate the temperature so that the water bath does not exceed 175°F during cooking. The terrine is done when the juices run clear, about 1½ hours, or when internal temperature reads 150°F.

Remove and allow to cool. Decorate per suggestions on page 76. Finish with port wine aspic (*recipe on page 84*). Serve not sooner than the following day in the terrine in which it was cooked. Distribute slices on individual serving plates by slicing downward with a sharp knife and lifting out each portion.

PHEASANT WITH SAUERKRAUT

The first rule of pheasant cooking, in every case, is that the bird is cooked slowly, and moistly. Secondly, regardless of the cooking method employed, the chef must pay homage to the flavors — of the meat, seasonings, and the resulting liquor — and the foundation for that is always a good stock.

1 pheasant, jointed into four pieces
4 tablespoons olive oil
2 tablespoons butter
1 onion, finely chopped
2 pounds sauerkraut, rinsed and drained
2 cups white wine

2 cups Madeira
2 cups veal stock
Salt and pepper
2 cups cooked, finger-sized spicy link sausage (Holsteiner kochwurst or other), cut in 2-inch slices
1 teaspoon caraway seeds

In a sauté pan melt half the oil and butter and lightly brown the onions. Add the sauerkraut, the wines and the stock, cover, and simmer for 45 minutes. Add salt and pepper to taste.

In a skillet melt the remaining butter and oil and brown the bird pieces over low heat, turning frequently for 20 minutes.

In a low-sided baking dish with a lid, add the sauerkraut, the pheasant pieces, the caraway seed, and then the sausage. Cover and bake in a preheated 375°F oven for 30 minutes, then serve.

Grilled Pheasant Stuffed with Dill and Goat Cheese

The great American staple, the backyard barbecue, is but one example of how the scope of cooking pheasant has expanded.
A magnificent illustration of this is pheasant stuffed with a mixture of dill and goat cheese under the skin, and brushed with lime butter on top.

2 pheasant, split in half, top to bottom
8 ounces mild goat cheese
4 ounces butter, softened
4 tablespoons fresh dill, chopped
Salt and pepper
2 cups lime butter

LIME BUTTER
Blend the following:
2 cups butter, softened
1 cup white wine
¼ cup heavy cream
3 tablespoons lime zest, diced
Juice of 5 key limes, seeded

Build a fire an hour before you want to cook, and allow enough coals to cook for 45 minutes.

Split the pheasant down the backbone using kitchen shears, and following the incision of a paring knife, cut through the breastbone to make 2 even halves.

Combine the cheese, butter and dill in a food processor or blend by hand until smooth. Add salt and pepper to taste. Carefully loosen the skin over the breast of the pheasant, and stuff the cheese mixture between the skin and meat, patting the mixture out evenly. Coat each pheasant piece with the lime butter.

When the coals are glowing, and all flame has subsided, arrange the grill 4 inches from the coals and place the birds skin down for 1 minute. Using a spatula, turn the birds and keep turning every 10 minutes until done, about 45 minutes. Continue to baste the breasts of the birds after each turn with the lime butter.

Pheasant Stir-fry with Chinese Noodles

The farm-raised birds of today are uniform, young, and carefully picked.
Because of that they offer more scope to the ambitious chef, and can be used in ways that their wild-caught cousins cannot.

2 pheasant, skinned, boned, and sliced into ½-inch cubes
2-3 tablespoons vegetable oil
I cup unsalted cashews, roughly broken
8 small dried red chilies (arbol, cascabel or similar)
I teaspoon fresh ginger, peeled and minced
2 green onions with tops, chopped in ½-inch lengths
I cup fresh snow peas
I cup Chinese cabbage, shredded
2 cups Chinese noodles, soft

MARINADE
I tablespoon dry sherry
I teaspoon soy sauce
I egg white
I tablespoon cornstarch

SAUCE
I teaspoon cornstarch
¼ cup stock (chicken, game or veal)
I teaspoon chili paste with garlic
2 tablespoons soy sauce
I tablespoon dry sherry
I teaspoon each of red wine vinegar, sugar, and sesame oil

Combine the sherry, soy sauce, egg white and cornstarch in a bowl and stir to dissolve the starch. Add the pheasant cubes and toss well to coat. Marinate for 20 minutes.

In a large bowl, make a sauce from the cornstarch and chicken stock, adding the chili paste, soy sauce, sherry, vinegar, sugar and sesame oil, blend thoroughly and set aside. Prepare the Chinese noodles and cover with foil and set aside in a warm oven awaiting final assembly.

Bring a wok or large frying pan to medium-high heat and add I tablespoon of the vegetable oil, swirling to coat the pan evenly. Add the chilies and cashews, stir and toss until the cashews take on a darker color, about 3 minutes.

(Recipe continued on page 32.)

PHEASANT STIR-FRY WITH CHINESE NOODLES (CONTINUED)

Remove to a bowl. Reserve the oil. Add an additional tablespoon of oil, swirling again to coat the pan. Using a slotted spoon remove a third of the pheasant cubes from the marinade, and cook them in the wok, raking them up and down the sides and turning to achieve an even color, and cook for about 5 minutes. Add a splash of oil as needed, and repeat with the remaining pheasant.

Return all the cooked ingredients to the wok including the ginger and green onions, increase the heat and toss until coated. Quickly add the snow peas. Stir the bowl of sauce once more to mix, then add it all at once to the pan and continue tossing until it thickens, about 2 minutes. Then add the Chinese cabbage and toss once. Serve immediately over the noodles.

PHEASANT CACCIATORE

Roasting the birds with the cavities stuffed forces the steamed vegetables to share flavors with the meat, and greatly improves each.

2 pheasant, whole, skin on
½ cup extra-virgin olive oil
½ cup dry red wine
2 cups ripe tomatoes, quartered
1 cup onion, chopped

1 bell pepper, seeded and chopped
1 serrano chili, seeded and chopped (optional)
1 cup mushrooms, thinly sliced
Salt and pepper

Rub the birds inside and out with the olive oil, then pour the excess oil in a bowl. Add the wine to this bowl. Salt and pepper both birds, inside and out.

Put the tomatoes, onion, peppers and mushrooms in a bowl and sprinkle with a pinch of salt. Then add them to the wine and oil mixture, and soak for 15 minutes.

Separate the vegetables from the wine, and pour the wine/oil mixture into an open roasting pan large enough to hold both birds. Stuff both birds loosely with the vegetable mixture, and close the cavity securely with small poultry skewers and a length of cotton twine. In a preheated oven at 350°F cook the birds for 50 minutes in the roasting pan, basting and turning three times.

BRAISED PHEASANT IN MADEIRA AND JUNIPER BERRIES

Famous recipes each have their distinctive ingredients, but the common thread is a subtle shading across the flavor notes and textures of fruits and wines.
The tartness of orange or lemon, staggered against the abrupt and mellow juniper berry and carried along on a sea of port or Madeira, reaches a most sublime taste sensation.

1 pheasant, cleaned with skin on
2 tablespoons lard or vegetable oil
1 dozen small mushroom caps, sliced
3 small shallots, chopped
2 tablespoons butter

1 tablespoon arrowroot
2 cups Madeira wine
¼ teaspoon dried fennel seeds, crushed
12 juniper berries, bruised
1 small tangerine, peeled, seeded and sectioned

In a large sauté pan melt the lard over medium-high heat. Brown the bird, rolling and basting and browning on all sides for 15 minutes. Remove the bird but retain the lard in the pan. Stuff the cavity of the bird with the tangerine sections, and transfer to a braising pot with a tight fitting lid and keep warm.

Combine the arrowroot and the Madeira in a small bowl. Return the sauté pan with remaining lard to medium heat. Add the butter and sauté the mushrooms and shallots, then gradually pour in the Madeira mixture, stirring constantly. Taste and season with salt and pepper. Add the fennel and the juniper berries and continue over low heat until warm. Remove from the heat.

Pour the wine mixture over the bird in the braising pot, cover, and cook for 25 minutes in a pre-heated 400°F oven without disturbing. Carve and serve with the pan juices poured over. This dish goes well with fried hominy, red currant jelly and asparagus.

Supremes of Pheasant with Sauce Bigarade

The Bigarade sauce used here with poached supremes is one of many plays on the tart/sweet wonder of the Seville oranges of Spain.
In a pinch the addition to your sauce of a few tablespoons of your best marmalade will bring a similar poignant contrast to the taste of the pheasant.

8 skinless, boneless pheasant breasts
½ cup white flour
Salt and pepper
1 teaspoon pâté salt (*recipe on page 88*)
2 tablespoons butter
2 tablespoons olive oil
2 cups Sauce Bigarade (*recipe follows*)
1 teaspoon white or other peppercorns, chopped

SAUCE BIGARADE
3 cups veal stock
½ cup orange juice
½ cup lemon juice
the rind of one orange, diced
2 tablespoons of sugar, caramelized in 5 tablespoons red wine vinegar
1½ tablespoons arrowroot
½ teaspoon pâté salt (*recipe on page 88*)
½ teaspoon cayenne pepper
Salt and pepper

To separate the breasts, or supremes, from the bird use a small knife, removing all fat and skin from the whole breast (making two split breasts per bird). Dust the supremes with the flour, salt, pepper and pâté salt and refrigerate until needed.

Prepare the Sauce Bigarade (*see page 38*).

Heat the butter with oil in a sauté pan over medium-high heat, but not smoking. Sauté the breasts 2 minutes per side; the meat will be resistant to the touch. Pour in the prepared sauce, and return to a simmer for an additional 2 minutes.

Remove the breasts to hot serving plates, reserving sauce in the pan. Add the chopped peppercorns to the sauce, raise the heat to bring the sauce to a quick boil, and spoon it over the pheasant supremes. Serve with broccoli. (*Recipe continued on page 38.*)

SUPREMES OF PHEASANT WITH SAUCE BIGARADE (CONTINUED)

Sauce Bigarade: In a small pan over high heat begin the reduction of the veal stock. After 5 minutes add the orange rind and continue reducing to 1 cup. In the meantime, in another small pan, caramelize the sugar by combing sugar and vinegar; stirring constantly over medium-high heat, reduce this mixture to a very thick syrup, about 2 tablespoons. This mixture will harden when cooled but can be easily returned to liquid state by immersing the pan in hot water.

In a bowl combine the orange juice, lemon juice, arrowroot, pâté salt, cayenne pepper and caramelized sugar. When the reduction of the stock to 1 cup is complete, slowly pour the juice mixture into the stock, stirring constantly over low heat. Taste and adjust for salt and pepper. Reheat the sauce in the roasting pan after the supremes have been withdrawn, and then spoon over the meat.

POTAGE DE FAISAN

The Prince of Wales had a dozen of his chums over for a pheasant shoot at Sandringham, his place in what was then known as Norfolk, the pheasant mecca of jolly olde England. On a golden September morning a hundred years ago the shooting party banged 3,114 birds and retired for a late, long lunch catered down from the great house. The Prince lifted a glass. "To the bird, the most excellent bird," he toasted, and ever since the pheasant has come down to us as a gaudy icon, the very epitome of both shooting sport and "haute cuisine."

2 cups pheasant meat, cooked and pared from bones
2 cups sherry
1 tablespoon arrowroot
2 tablespoons butter
2 small carrots, thinly sliced

2 shallots, thinly sliced
¼ teaspoon dried tarragon
2 cups gamebird fumet (*recipe on page 88*)
Salt and pepper

In a Dutch oven melt the butter and soften the carrots and shallots over low heat for 5 minutes. Add the tarragon, and continue to sauté without browning for 2 minutes.

In a food processor, combine the pheasant meat, the arrowroot, and the sherry and blend to a fine puree. Add this to the carrots and shallots in the Dutch oven, and then slowly pour in the game bird fumet. Bring the mixture to a simmer, remove from the heat and allow to stand 5 minutes. Adjust the seasoning and serve.

POACHER'S POT PIE

The high art of André Soltner at Lutèce and the sturdy pheasant pot pie of humbler provenance both rely on an easy form of the pastry called pâté brisée.

2 pheasant (for 4 small pies)
2 tablespoons butter
2 tablespoons olive oil
1 clove garlic, crushed
4 cups veal stock or optional game fumet (*recipe on page 88*)

4 tablespoons arrowroot
1 cup Madeira
2 cups glazed baby onions (*recipe on page 87*)
2 cups sautéed mushrooms (*recipe on page 86*)
2 pounds of pâté brisée or puff pastry (*recipe on pages 90-91*)

Breast each bird and leave the breasts whole for the moment; then pare the meat off the legs and wings. Skin the meat and set aside. The bones and carcass will be useful for the optional game fumet. Discard the skin.

In an ovenproof pan glaze the onions and reserve. Dredge the pheasant breasts and meat lightly in flour, then sauté all the meat in the butter and oil briefly, just enough to bring color to the meat, but not cooking through, about 5 minutes. Remove the meat and slice the breasts crosswise into four pieces each.

In a small sauce pan warm the veal stock. In a small bowl combine the arrowroot and the Madeira and stir. When the arrowroot is dissolved, add this to the stock and remove from the heat. Continue stirring the stock until it thickens.

Fill each ovenproof serving dish with a selection of meat, onions and sautéed mushrooms, then add the thickened stock up to the lip of the dish. Remove the pastry from the refrigerator, roll out to ½-inch thickness, cut to size, and apply a pastry lid to each serving dish, and carve or punch a steam hole in the center of the lid. Refrigerate 30 minutes before baking.

In a preheated 450°F oven, bake the pies for 10 minutes, then reduce the heat to 400°F and continue cooking for 30 minutes or so, depending on the browning of the pastry.

QUAIL

"THIS IS SUPPOSED TO BE FUN"
– Julia Child

If you wanted quail in the first half of this century in America, you pretty well had to shoot it yourself. And on your own land. Birds just weren't available commercially and that fact may have added to the special allure and very high esteem of quail at the table. It was often joked that no one could eat a quail a day for a month, but the joke was that nobody had enough quail to challenge the proposition.

There was a time when men on horses with big running dogs could find over a hundred coveys in a day of hard hunting. On the Dougherty Ranch deep in the heart of the old Wild Horse Desert of South Texas I have spent many a day in the company of Ben Vaughan and John Harman, running behind dogs with names like Hector and Whoa Dammit, and enjoying the easy riding of Harman's big gaited horses. Ben would always praise the Lord and call it a pretty good morning when we found fifty coveys before lunch.

But the reality of quail hunting for most of us was walking fence rows with dad, watching birds flush quickly out of range, and then flit through a fence and around a briar patch, out of harm's way. As we peered across the pasture, the whistling of a cock bird on a wire fence, regrouping his covey, was a subtle comment on their sturdy independence.

Quail were so universally admired during my childhood that guests usually dropped whatever they were doing and came straight over when invited. I remember one evening my daddy returned with fresh birds and an intention to braise them in celery and sherry in his old French brazier's pot.

With hardly a raised eyebrow, Miss Imma Hogg, my mother and a few other venerable old dames upped stakes and moved their museum meeting into our kitchen. They sat around that long, red painted table, sipping bourbon old-fashioneds out of silver cups, and planning and plotting the creation of what is now the Bayou Bend Museum to the sizzle and bouquet of quail wafting across the kitchen.

In the country, quail were invariably smothered or roasted over open charcoal fires. Many restaurants along the

Mexican border offered wild trapped birds, and developed a special following. I have seen photographs commemorating the convocation of a rump session of the Texas Legislature at the Cadillac Bar & Grill during prohibition.

There they were, forty venerable lawmen, perhaps not a quorum, thumbs in vest pockets, lined up along the old oak bar. Some are smiling, one or two have a fist raised on high as though to drive home their oratorical demand for justice to the people they represented back home.

Some say they were not there for the quail. But I say it is an unseemly slur on the integrity of the legislature of the great State of Texas to suggest that the motivation behind this patriotic assembly had anything whatsoever to do with the relative ease of obtaining whiskey in Mexico.

During the sixties Americans began to come together on the questions of haute cuisine, cuisine bourgeois and the puritan "fear of food." Many of the world's great cuisines gradually became accessible and exciting for home chefs. Julia Child was at the front of this revolution, and she did it all by hard work and a simple unwillingness to take herself too seriously. After all, as she has said many times, "this is supposed to be fun."

I have adapted her wild rice crouton to make the quail on toast offered in these pages. The quail is so versatile that it tolerates this sort of adjustment without rumpling a feather.

I remember a time in 1977 when I was staying at the Stanford Court Hotel in San Francisco on a business trip. On my arrival I had set out in search of the hotel bar. As I rounded the corner I was confronted by a very large man with a shining bald head and great bear paws for hands stuck out at his sides. We nodded to each other in the passageway, and I muttered something like, "You sure do look like James Beard!"

For those of you who knew him, you will recognize that such a comment was all the invitation he needed. "It's a damn good thing," he roared back, "because, that's who I am."

We had a drink and he wanted to talk about garlic and his mission of awakening America's dining class to the forbidden joys of the strongest onion.

Finally I asked how much garlic a man in his position could urge on a slightly suspicious public, taking into consideration the bounds of good taste and commonly accepted standards of decency in our time.

"How much?" he bellowed, "Acres of it," he said, and we bid good day.

At the other end of America the great restaurants were bringing food closer to the people. André Soltner of the restaurant Lutèce was creative and brilliant in this regard, but very modest and congenial. He offered a quail pâté that was made of whole birds, bone in, rolled out on the table in a formless pastry that can only be described as "down home," and his pastry is still very much in use today.

Before quail could be bought over the telephone wire as today, they "shot birds" from mules as the dogs ranged across the rolling savannahs dotted with live oak way down in southern Alabama. In the late fifties Lee J. Cobb, the movie star, was hunting with John Blaffer and a crowd of old University of Virginia alumni. Cobb was already a celebrity by this time, and he was no longer quite so lithe as in his college days.

After each covey rise he found it more difficult to swing up on his mule, and eventually took to walking until he could find a tree stump to give him a boost up. By the end of the day he was walking as much as riding and the strain was talking its toll.

When the day was done, and the mules and dogs were put away, the party retired to the sitting room in the great house, with their fancy guest. Around a fire of pecan logs, with their long boots hiked up against the fire screen, they waited for the pot roast to come done.

Promptly the steward, named Uncle, rolled out a polished oak decanter box and began passing the drinks around.

Before long you could hear the sound of ice tinkling in short glasses and there was a joke or two about the shooting. Finally Cobb began weaving his tales, and the floor was pretty much his.

He stretched his long, tired legs, and leaned forward in his chair. He grimaced as he touched his back with one hand, and set his drinking glass on the decanter box. Cobb turned to the steward, and in his best imitation of a Kentucky Colonel whisper, he asked, "Uncle, I am shore brought down in the back from all that walking and climbing back on that mule. If we do find some birds tomorrow, do you think I could just shoot off that mule?"

Uncle looked at him with a twinkle in his eye and scratched the back of his fingers across his throat, "Well, surely you could, Mr. Cobb," he said slowly, "But jest one'st."

BRAISED QUAIL WITH CELERY

My father used to braise quail in celery and sherry in his old French brazier's pot.
That pot had quite a reputation; it could hold four ducks or a dozen quail, and had a specially designed lid that directed the condensed cooking fluids back down onto the birds.
The enamel was a brilliant flame orange fading into red. It's thirty years on, and I still use that pot for quail and celery.

8 whole quail, split down the back
2 cups dry sherry
2 tablespoons lemon juice
Salt and pepper
8 celery stalk center stems with leaves
2 quarts water to parboil the celery

4 tablespoons olive oil
1 tablespoon butter
1 quart veal stock
Beurre manie
1½ tablespoons arrowroot
1½ tablespoons butter, kneaded

Mix the sherry and lemon juice with salt and pepper and turn the open quail in this mixture; marinate for 2 hours.

Strip the celery stalks down, discarding the coarse outer leaves for some other purpose, and retain the pristine inner heart, about 3 stalks with leaves, and tie each of these bundles tightly with kitchen twine. In a large pot bring the water to a boil, plunge the celery, allow the water to return to a boil; then remove the celery and pour off the water.

In a six-quart braising dish, bring the olive oil and butter to high heat on the stove. Remove the birds from the marinade, reserving the marinade, and sauté the birds in the oil and butter, turning them quickly with a spoon to achieve a slight tightening of the skin and a blush of color, about 10 minutes. Remove the pan from the heat, and remove the birds from the cooking oils. Wrap each bird around a bundle of parboiled celery and close with a short length of cotton string. Return the birds to the braising pan, add the stock and the reserved marinade, reaching about halfway up the sides of the birds. Bring this braise to a simmer, cover with a tight-fitting lid, and then place into a preheated 350°F oven. Baste twice during 45 minutes. The birds are done when the juices run clear and the thigh is tender when squeezed. *(Recipe continued on page 50.)*

Braised Quail with Celery (continued)

Remove the braising dish from the oven, and lift out each bird and celery combination intact. After removing the string, reserve the birds in a warm place. Return the braising dish to the top of the stove at high heat, and reduce the liquid to 1 cup. Blend the beurre manie into the reduced cooking liquid, and heat thoroughly, allowing the sauce to thicken slightly. Adjust the seasonings before serving in a sauceboat.

Roast Quail in Grape Leaves

In the old days invitations to a quail dinner were scarce and heavily coveted. One might expect the linen tablecloths, napkins, and the good silver.
And in the days before everything was frozen, an invitation to a quail supper had the immediacy of a command performance.

8 quail, whole
Salt and pepper
⅓ cup Spanish olive oil

8 slices bacon
24 large grape leaves, washed
Cotton string

Rub each bird inside and out with the olive oil, then salt and pepper the birds. Remove the stems from the grape leaves and place one leaf over each breast, and add 1 or 2 more leaves to completely encircle the bird. Wrap each bird with a piece of bacon, and secure with loops of string, one at the legs and one at the breast.

Preheat the oven to 450°F and arrange the birds in an open, ovenproof dish and roast breast up for 15 minutes. Remove the string, bacon and grape leaves and return the birds breast up for 5 minutes to brown in 400°F heat. Serve over fried bread.

Split Quail Grilled with Pepper Sauce

In northern Mexico quail were invariably roasted over open charcoal fires. At the old Cadillac Bar and Grill in the little town of Nuevo Laredo the quail were displayed against a tile wall, impaled on spits made from green mesquite switches, and rubbed with serrano peppers and garlic. The birds were served amidst bowls of Mandarin oranges and carambola fruit brought up from the South, and daubed with a green poblano pepper sauce that was never hot, but always tasted fully of pepper.

8 quail, whole and split down the front
8 large cloves of garlic, peeled
8 serrano peppers, fresh and green,
4 tablespoons olive oil

Salt and pepper
2 tablespoons butter kneaded with ½ teaspoon of ground cumin
16 small bamboo skewers
2 cups Poblano pepper sauce (*recipe on page 84*), optional

The most important aspect of grilling over an open fire is the condition of the coals. The fire must have been burning for at least one hour for the coals to acquire the proper deep heat and absence of visible flames.

Lay each split bird skin up on a cutting board and press firmly with the palm of your hand, breaking the breastbone, and flattening the bird. Carefully inspect each bird for bone shards. Rub both sides of the birds with the olive oil and salt and pepper. The skewers, two per bird, are thrust first through the shoulder side, then through one garlic clove and one serrano pepper, and then through the second shoulder. The second skewer passes unadorned through the legs. This is necessary to keep the birds flat during grilling.

Rake or drag the still-flaming coals to the opposite side, and cook these delicate quail only a few minutes per side over bright coals, depending on wind conditions.

Place the birds breast down for 3 to 4 minutes, squelching any flame flare up underneath the birds with a splash of water. Turn the birds over and continue cooking for 5 minutes, covering with a lid if the wind is high, and brushing 2 times with cumin butter. The Poblano pepper sauce, which is optional, should be prepared in advance. Serve a dollop of sauce beside the birds with fresh fruit.

QUAIL ON TOAST

For service and presentation of this dish, add a few sprinklings of Parmesan cheese over the top,
baste with the pan juices and allow the cheese to take on a crunch before serving. Serve the assembly with a flashy salad.

3 quail, split in half from top to bottom, boned
½ cup butter
Salt and freshly ground pepper
6 large slices of homemade white bread, ½-inch thick

1 egg
½ cup Swiss cheese, grated
2 cups wild rice, braised and ready to eat (*recipe on page 86*)
2 tablespoons Parmesan cheese, grated

Prepare the toast, or "croutons," by trimming the bread slices into an oval shape slightly larger than each bird. Sauté the bread slices in half of the butter until they will hold their form, but are not brown. They will take on a nice color in the final cooking. Beat the egg and add the Swiss cheese and blend this combination with the wild rice. Divide the rice mixture into six equal portions and mound these on each piece of fried toast and reserve.

Split the quail in half lengthwise, using shears to cut down the backbone and then down the breast. Remove any shards of bone, brush both sides of the birds with melted butter, and season lightly with salt and pepper. In a preheated 325°F oven, broil the birds breast down in a roasting pan for 7 minutes, turn, and continue broiling for another 7 minutes. Remove the birds and reserve the cooking juices.

Place each piece of toast with its mound of wild rice in the same roasting pan and press one bird, breast side up, over each assembly.

Preheat the oven to 400°F and bake the assembled birds in the roasting pan for 20 minutes, being careful not to scorch. They are done when the juices run clear, or an internal temperature is 145°F (the thighs will be tender when squeezed). Top with Parmesan cheese and baste with pan juices.

Quail Broiled with Apricots and Figs

From the old Le Pavillion in New York I have adopted a stuffed quail that is broiled and served with apricots and figs.
It is essential Pierre Franey, although he might not recognize it.
The strength of the recipe is in his surprise addition of selected herb seeds, designed to complete the flavor cycle of fruit and meats.

8 quail, partially boned
2 tablespoons whole coriander, crushed
½ cup gin
1 cup dried apricots
1 cup dried figs
1 cup veal stock
1 cup ground turkey sausage
6 tablespoons olive oil, divided
3 tablespoons butter, divided

1 cup chopped onions
4 tablespoons golden raisins
½ teaspoon ground cumin
½ teaspoon ground cinnamon
Salt and pepper
2 tablespoons fresh thyme (or 1 teaspoon dried)
1 tablespoon rubbed sage
2 cups couscous, cooked (or small-grain rice, parboiled)

Soak the crushed coriander seed in gin for 15 minutes. Slice the dried apricots and figs narrowly, four slices per fruit, and add to the gin and coriander marinade. Add veal stock and continue marinating the apricots and figs, stirring, frequently.

Prepare the stuffing by sautéing the sausage in 2 tablespoons oil and 1 tablespoon butter over low heat, then add the onions until the latter are softened, but not browned. Add the raisins, cumin, cinnamon, and salt and pepper and continue cooking for 5 minutes over low heat. Remove from the stove and allow the stuffing to cool.

Salt and pepper the interior of each bird, and then fill each bird with the stuffing mixture. Leave the birds untrussed, but flatten slightly with the palm of your hand to establish their shape.

Preheat the oven to 325°F. Add the remaining butter and 4 tablespoons oil to a large baking dish, and then

(Recipe continued on page 58.)

QUAIL BROILED WITH APRICOTS AND FIGS (CONTINUED)

introduce the quail, turning each one to coat. Sprinkle each quail with thyme and sage, and roll again to distribute. Add the apricots, figs, coriander and their marinade to the baking dish, and place each quail breast side down, in single row around the pan.

At this point begin cooking the couscous following package instructions. Place the baking pan on the second rack from the top of the oven, and with the oven door ajar, broil the birds for about 8 minutes, until the birds begin to brown. Turn the quail breast up and continue broiling and basting for 8 minutes more.

When the birds are brown, cover tightly with foil and remove the pan to the lowest rack of the oven, and continue baking at 400°F for an additional 8 minutes with the door closed. Remove the birds carefully and keep warm while you prepare a couscous bed on each plate. Cover the grains with a share of pan drippings, apricot and figs, place the birds over the bed of fruit and serve.

SAVORY QUAIL MILANESE

One of the joys of pursuing culinary interests around the world has always been, for me, the excitement of encounter.
Nothing stays the same for long in gastronomy, and the wave of constant invention brought on by new brains, and eager challengers to the old ways is always a hoot.

8 quail, boned
2 cups spinach
1 shallot, chopped
1 garlic clove, chopped
2 slices bacon, diced
1 cup mushrooms, diced
3 tablespoons butter
1 cup chicken livers
2 tablespoons sunflower seeds, browned in butter

RISOTTO
4 tablespoons butter
1 onion, finely diced
1 cup risotto rice (such as Arborio)
3 cups veal stock
Salt and pepper

Blanch the spinach in boiling water for 2 minutes, then drain and squeeze dry. In a sauté pan melt the butter. Fry the bacon, shallots, garlic and mushrooms in the butter over medium heat until soft. Add the chicken livers and sunflower seeds and shake the pan for 4 minutes more, giving color to the livers.

Chop the bacon mixture roughly and blend in the chopped spinach. Add salt and pepper. Stuff each quail with the mixture, and place the birds in a buttered roasting pan. In a preheated oven at 400°F roast the birds for 12 minutes, turning twice.

Next, prepare the risotto: Melt the butter in a sauce pan and sauté the onion until soft. Add the rice and stir for 3 minutes. Add a few tablespoons of the stock and stir until absorbed. Continue adding stock in this manner until the rice is tender and the stock has been absorbed, about 20 minutes. Serve the quail over a bed of risotto.

Flambé of Quail with Apples and Calvados

Paul Bocuse, when he owned a restaurant at Colonges-au-Mt-d'Or, near Lyon, was a great showman. He would grab an apple and a bottle of Calvados and proclaim that the two grew up together and were made from one another, and therefore intended for each other, eternally!
With a wink he would whisper, " . . . they came to dinner together, but they need a little crème fraîche to soothe their tempestuous passions."

4 quail, split in half lengthwise
Salt and freshly ground pepper to taste
½ cup plus 2 tablespoons butter
1 cup button mushrooms, thinly sliced
1 teaspoon dried, ground thyme
4 tablespoons chopped shallots

4 tablespoons chopped parsley
2 cloves garlic, minced
2 tart, yellow-skinned apples, skin on, seeded and sliced
½ cup Calvados (apple brandy)
1 cup crème fraîche (or heavy cream)

Sauté the apple slices gently in 2 tablespoons of butter for not more than 5 minutes. Remove and set aside for the flambé.

Season the quail halves with salt and pepper. Melt ½ cup butter in a large, deep sauté pan, add the quail halves, breast side up, and mushrooms; cook over low heat for 5 minutes. Crumble half of the dried thyme and sprinkle over the birds.

Turn the birds breast down, and continue to sauté over low heat for an additional 5 minutes. Add the remaining thyme over the birds. Add the shallots, garlic and parsley, and stir gently. Turn the birds breast up, add the apple slices and continue to sauté over low heat for another 5 minutes.

When the flesh of the birds is firm they are nearly done.

Sprinkle the birds and apples with the Calvados and ignite. Gently lift the quail halves with a slotted wooden spoon to distribute the Calvados. After the flame subsides, extinguish by placing a lid on the pan. Remove the quail, apples, shallots, parsley and mushrooms. Arrange the quail on serving plates surrounded by the apples and mushrooms and keep warm while the sauce is prepared.

Return the sauté pan to the stove, and over low heat add the crème fraîche and continue stirring over low heat until the mixture thickens slightly. Correct the seasonings, and ladle one spoonful over each bird. Pour remaining sauce in a sauceboat. Serve with sprigs of fresh parsley.

CASSEROLE OF QUAIL WITH GARLIC AND ROSEMARY

James Beard loved his recipe for "forty garlic chicken" and revised and adjusted it over the years to reach its present incarnation, for which he is justly renowned. The version here takes into account the different cooking times of chicken versus quail, the delicate quality of quail meat, and the requirements of roasted garlic. I mention forty cloves here out of respect for old Beard, and for the nostalgia of his golden rule on garlic, "the more the better."

½ cup olive oil
8 whole quail, partially boned
1 cup celery stalks, cut in strips
1 cup onions, chopped
40 unpeeled garlic cloves, separated
¼ cup chopped parsley

2 tablespoons fresh rosemary, bruised
½ teaspoon salt
Freshly ground black pepper
¼ teaspoon nutmeg
½ cup brandy
4 rosemary sprigs, 6 inches each

Put the oil in a heavy casserole and add the celery, onions, garlic cloves, parsley, rosemary, salt and pepper. Seal the casserole with foil in addition to the lid and set the pot in a 375°F oven for 45 minutes.

Remove the casserole and add the quail, turning each bird to coat evenly with the mixture. Pour in the brandy and mix well. Replace the foil and lid and return to the oven for another 30 minutes.

Remove the lid and foil and allow the quail to brown for a final 15 minutes, basting if necessary. The quail are done when the breasts are firm to the touch.

Serve directly from the casserole, each quail with a rosemary spear, a helping of garlic cloves, and a torn crust of baguette. Squeeze some garlic from the husks and spread it on the bread.

Quail Pâté en Croûte

The availability of fully boned farm-raised birds has exploded America's culinary opportunities in regard to these venerable birds.

10 quail, skinned and boned
4 slices unsmoked bacon, chopped into 1-inch pieces
1 sprig fresh thyme (or a pinch of dried)
1 cup of foie gras or chicken livers, marinated in brandy
½ cup lean veal, cubed
½ cup green scallions with tops, chopped
4 tablespoons brandy
1 tablespoon pâté salt (*recipe on page 88*)

2 eggs, gently beaten
1 teaspoon salt
Freshly ground pepper
½ cup sunflower seeds, browned in butter
Butter for greasing mold
3 pounds Pâté Brisée (*recipe on page 91*)
1¼-quart pâté mold with drop sides, about 13 inches long
Madeira aspic to finish (*recipe on page 83*)

Separate the breast meat from the leg and thigh meat, there should be 1½ cups of each; set the leg and thigh meat aside. Slice the breasts into thirds lengthwise and set aside. In a pan over medium heat, sauté the bacon, add the thyme, and continue cooking for about 3 minutes. Add the foie gras and the veal, continuing to sauté for 5 minutes. Add the scallions, and continue cooking for 1 minute. Pour half the brandy over the meat in the sauté pan and ignite.

When the flame subsides discard the thyme. In a large mixing bowl combine the leg and thigh meat, the sautéed mixture, add the pâté salt, eggs and the remaining brandy, and mix. Put the mixture in a processor and whirl briefly, not more than 30 seconds. Add salt and pepper, and refrigerate for 1 hour.

Grease the inside of the assembled mold. Roll out the pastry to a half-inch thick. Line the bottom and sides with the pastry and fold over the top of the sides to form a rim and provide a platform for joining the top. (*Additional suggestions for this technique are on page 78.*)

Using a large spoon, paddle the browned sunflower seeds evenly into the ground forcemeat mixture. Place

(*Recipe continued on page 66.*)

Quail Pâté en Croûte (continued)

half the forcemeat in the pâté mold, then the reserved breast slices in an even layer, then cover with the remaining forcemeat. Paint the rim of the pastry case with beaten egg, then fold a sheet of pastry over the top. Use the back of a fork to seal the edges together. Cut openings for the steam to escape and insert funnels to keep the pathway open during cooking. Brush the top with beaten egg. Roll out the trimmed pieces of pastry and cut design emblems, such as small leaves, to be applied to the top. Brush again with beaten egg.

Bake in a preheated oven at 425°F for 15 minutes, then reduce the heat to 350°F and bake for another 30 minutes or so. Cover with foil if browning appears before an internal temperature of 150°F is reached. Drop the sides of the mold, retain the foil cover, and allow the sides to take on color at 375°F for 10 minutes.

When the pâté is cold fill with Madeira aspic (*recipe on page 83*). Serve with tailgate mayonnaise (*recipe on page 85*).

FERNAND POINT'S QUAIL

*Renowned and revered chefs made it very clear that the delicate, slightly hidden flavor of quail was worthy of investigation.
In their high-profile professional life they loudly proclaimed that its great flavor was brought to robust identity
by its combination with stock, fruit flavors, and a thoughtful hand at the stove.*

4 quail, boned
4 tablespoons butter
8 slices bacon
4 garlic cloves, crushed
½ teaspoon dried thyme
½ cup veal stock

½ cup Madeira
2 tablespoons brandy
1 tablespoon butter, cut into bits, and kneaded with scant
   (½ teaspoon) arrowroot
4 tablespoons chopped parsley

In a sauté pan melt the butter over medium heat. Add the quail, bacon, garlic and thyme. Cover and cook for 12 minutes over medium heat, turning and basting the birds frequently.

Remove the birds to a serving platter and discard the bacon. Deglaze the sauté pan with the veal stock over high heat, stirring and scraping until the liquid is reduced to 4 tablespoons. Reduce the heat, add the Madeira and brandy and continue stirring. Add the butter bits and stir until the consistency thickens. Spoon the sauce over the birds and sprinkle with the chopped parsley.

ALABAMA POT ROASTED QUAIL WITH PECANS AND BOURBON

They're close to the soil, they're rich as Croesus and everybody loves them. How many people do you know like that?
The very thought of the glorious Bobwhite whistling in an Alabama pea patch is an image to conjure.
But it must be said in the same starstruck breath, that a simple pot roast of quail was always the highest culinary cotton in the Deep South.

8 quail, whole
Salt and paprika
4 tablespoons butter
4 tablespoons olive oil
½ cup chopped parsley
1 teaspoon rubbed sage
1 teaspoon freshly ground black pepper
½ cup pecans, lightly chopped

1 cup veal stock
1 cup Bourbon whiskey
Juice of 1 lemon
3 teaspoons Worcestershire sauce
½ cup pecans, ground to a coarse powder
3 tablespoons butter, flaked
Salt and pepper to taste

Dust the quail with salt and paprika, trussing the feet together, and the wings back. Sauté all the birds in 4 tablespoons each of butter and olive oil until brown on all sides and remove.

Chop the parsley, sage, black pepper and pecan parts together, and in a small bowl blend with a few tablespoons of the veal stock. Place a tablespoon of this stuffing in each bird and reserve the balance for coating the bird upon serving.

Put the stuffed birds, the remaining veal stock, whiskey, lemon juice, Worcestershire sauce and powdered pecans into a large covered casserole. Simmer for 1 hour over very low heat. Turn the birds every 15 minutes.

The birds are done when the breast pierces easily and the juice runs clear. Remove the birds and keep warm. Over high heat, boil the pan juices, scraping constantly until the mixture is reduced to 1 cup. Reduce the heat to the lowest setting, and whisk in the butter flakes, stirring until the sauce thickens. Add salt and pepper as needed.

Return the birds to the pot, and roll them in the sauce, warming and coating them. Serve in shallow bowls with fresh green beans with the remaining pecan and parsley stuffing spread on top of each bird, and the pot juices poured over.

Smothered Quail Casserole

As open hunting land slipped away from the face of rural America, in its place the long arm of commerce rose up to take an interest in matters gustatory, including farm-raised birds. Quail, which had been pushed off the prairies, were showing up as the proud product of a new cottage industry. The great chefs in New York discovered farm-raised birds on Long Island, and bird breeders from California to Carolina began to adapt their product to telemarketing.

8 quail, boned
Scant flour for dusting
2 tablespoons olive oil
¼ pound butter
3 shallots, diced
1 cup veal stock
1 cup dry sherry

½ teaspoon dill weed
½ teaspoon dried rosemary
1 rib of celery with leaves, finely chopped
2 tablespoons parsley, chopped
1 cup crème fraîche
Salt and pepper to taste
2 teaspoons Hungarian paprika

Split the quail lengthwise into halves; lightly salt and pepper and dust each half with the flour. Melt the butter and olive oil in a large sauté pan or skillet, add the diced shallots and sauté over low heat. After 2 minutes add the quail, and increase the heat, turning the birds often until well browned.

Combine the stock, sherry, dill, rosemary, celery, and half the parsley and pour into the sauté pan over the browned quail. Cover with a lid, and simmer over low heat for 15 minutes.

Reduce the heat, add the crème fraîche, salt and pepper. Stir, and continue simmering for 3 minutes. Sprinkle the paprika over the birds, and remove to a serving plate with the remaining parsley over and the sauce at the side.

BUILDING THE BALLOTINE OF PHEASANT

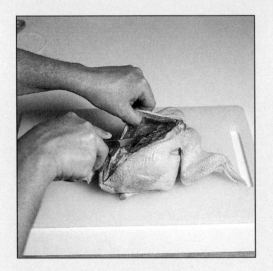  

1.
Skin each whole pheasant, beginning
with a midline cut down the backbone.
Work around the wing and leg, dislocat-
ing the joint of each with the tip of a
small knife. Stop when you reach the
breastbone or sternum on one side, and
repeat the process on the other side.

2.
Holding the carcass aloft, carefully slice
through the cartilaginous material that
connects the skin to the breastbone,
allowing the skin and meat to fall free.
Pare the meat from the legs and wings,
discarding the bones.

3.
Arrange the pheasant, skin side down,
meat up. Fill the cavity between the two
breasts with leg and wing meat scraped
from the bone. Spoon half of the
sausage mixture over the exposed meat,
and spread evenly.

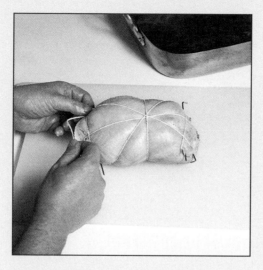

4.

Roll the ballotine from the tail toward
the head.

5.

Fold over and secure the flaps at the
ends with small poultry skewers and
even out the sides of the roll, lacing the
ballotine carefully with cotton string.
Cook in a shallow roasting pan with 2
tablespoons of butter over moderate
heat (350°F) turning several times and
basting with a spoon.

6.

When the ballotine has a rich brown
color it is done. Allow to cool before
removing skewers and string. Slice trans-
versely into ½-inch serving size slices,
half a bird per guest.

DECORATING THE PHEASANT TERRINE

I.

The forcemeat should be carefully spooned into the ceramic terrine, packing slightly to avoid air holes, and not filling beyond the lower inside lip of the terrine.

2.

Cover the terrine with foil, and the form-fitting lid over the foil. Put the terrine in a bain marie or shallow pan with one inch of boiling water. Temperature readings taken in the bain marie during cooking should not exceed 175°F. Adjust the oven temperature downward from 325°F if necessary.

3.

Measure and carefully slice the vegetables intended to be used for decoration, in this case, scallions, thin carrot triangles, and thin cross-sections of radish, which together will form the rosette.

4.

Soften 2 packages of powdered gelatin in 2 cups of stock. Stirring constantly, bring to a simmer and remove immediately from the heat. Soften the scallions and other vegetables by placing them in the hot aspic for 3 minutes, then withdraw and arrange the vegetables on the surface of the terrine. Add ½ cup of port wine to the bowl of aspic.

5.

Carefully spoon the remaining aspic over the design, being careful not to dislodge the design. Fill the aspic to the level of the lower lip only, allowing space for the lid.

6.

Allow to cool and refrigerate before serving the following day. Serve by cutting straight down with a sharp knife and lifting each serving to a separate plate.

CREATING THE QUAIL PÂTÉ EN CROÛTE

I.

The dough, called a pâté brisée, is made by mixing the flour, salt, and butter with your fingers until crumbly, then adding the egg and water combined. Knead the dough until it forms a ball and stop, do not overwork. Wrap the dough in plastic and refrigerate for an hour. (*See recipe on page 91.*)

2.

Divide the pastry ¾ for the body and ¼ for the lid and roll out the body to ½-inch thickness. Carefully lift the rolled pastry and fit it into the prepared mold. Use your fingers to seat the pastry in each corner. The pastry should overlap the rim by a ½-inch. Spoon in half of the forcemeat, then add the individual slices of breast meat in a single layer, followed by the remaining forcemeat.

3.

Brush the overlapping rim of the pastry case with a mixture of egg and water. Roll out the remaining pastry to form the lid, then gently lift the pastry lid into place.

4.

Use the tines of a fork to seal the edges of the pastry together, then trim away the excess dough. Roll out the bits of excess dough and cut design pieces, such as leaves or semi-circles, to decorate the lid, brushing with egg mixture before applying the design.

5.

Cut out two vent holes with a sharp knife, and insert foil funnels built around a pencil to allow the steam to escape. Brush the entire surface with egg mixture.

6.

Set in a preheated oven at 425°F for 15 minutes, then reduce to 350°F for an additional 30 minutes, cover with foil as browning appears. When an internal temperature of 150°F is reached drop the sides of the mold but retain the foil cover on top and return to the oven to brown the sides for 10 minutes at 375°F. Allow the pâté to cool. When cold remove the foil and pour Madeira aspic slowly through the vent holes to fill the pâté.

SPECIAL TREATMENT TO PROTECT THE MOISTNESS AND TO ENHANCE THE FLAVOR OF DELICATE BIRDS

  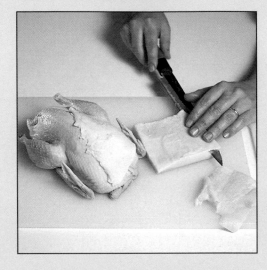

1.

The "caul" or omental fat of the pig is a traditional larding method for delicate birds. The caul should be draped over the bird, and wrapped around the legs and feet and around the back. Trim the excess. One caul can be cut to accommodate two pheasant or four quail.

2.

Bacon is a very useful larding method for quail. Here the unsmoked bacon strips are laid lengthwise across the breast, and secured with cotton twine running around the bird.

3.

To bard a pheasant use strips or sheets of pork fatback sliced as thinly as possible, but of sufficient length to cover the breast of the bird. The larding fat is then tied in place around the bird using cotton string.

4.

Stuffing a split pheasant with a savory mixture (dill and goat cheese in this picture) is done by lifting the skin slightly along the line of the sternum, and packing the space between the skin and the meat with stuffing. Push the material as far back as possible without tearing the skin, and then apply slight pressure with your hand across the skin to hold the mixture in place.

5.

Breasting a pheasant to obtain supremes. Place the bird breast up and slice down along the breast bone. Using the tip of the knife work against the rib bones from top to bottom to separate both meat and skin from the carcass. Peel back the skin.

6.

Veal stock for game bird cookery is the incomparable sauce obtained from the reduction of 10 quarts of water and 18 pounds of browned veal knuckle and shank bones, blended with onions, carrots and bay leaves to a mere 5 quarts of brown stock, known as "brun estouffade." The recipe may be reduced proportionately.

Supporting Recipes

Aspics & Sauces

Port Wine Sauce

1½ cups Port wine
1 teaspoon shallots, minced fine
¼ teaspoon dried thyme
Juice of 2 small oranges, seeded
Scant lemon juice

¼ teaspoon grated orange rind
Salt and cayenne pepper to taste
1 cup veal stock
1 scant tablespoon arrowroot

Over a hot fire reduce to half a generous cup of port wine, to which has been added the shallot, thyme, orange juice, lemon juice, orange rind, and a few grains of salt and cayenne to taste. Add 1 cup of good veal stock to which has been added the arrowroot stirred in a little port wine. Boil once, skim, and let simmer 5 minutes longer before straining into a sauceboat.

Madeira Aspic for Quail Pâté en Croûte

1 cup veal stock or game fumet (*recipe on page 88*)
½ cup Madeira

1 packet powdered gelatin

Reduce 1 cup of stock by half. Add gelatin that has been previously softened in a few tablespoons of the Madeira. Bring to a boil, stirring constantly, then set aside to cool over a bed of ice. Just before it sets, pour in the remaining Madeira and stir. Pour this into the cooled terrine through a tiny funnel and refrigerate for 2 hours before serving.

Port Wine Aspic

2 packages powdered gelatin
2 cups veal stock
½ cup Port wine

Soften gelatin in the stock. Stirring constantly, bring to a simmer and remove immediately from the heat. After the mixture has cooled slightly, but before it begins to set, add the port wine.

Poblano Pepper Sauce

2 tablespoons olive oil
4 poblano peppers (or large green bell peppers)
½ cup onions, chopped
2 tablespoons garlic, chopped

I teaspoon salt
I jalapeno pepper, seeded
2 teaspoons freshly ground black pepper
2 cups stock

Roast the poblano peppers in an open roasting pan in a 375°F oven turning several times, about 15 minutes. Peel off the skin and coarsely chop. Place the chopped pepper in stock together with the onions, garlic, jalapeno and black pepper and boil for 3 minutes. Puree the mixture in a processor, adding the heavy cream to reach the consistency of heavy mustard.

TAILGATE MAYONNAISE FOR PHEASANT TERRINE OR QUAIL PÂTÉ

I egg plus I yolk, broken
I tablespoon mustard, Dijon style
I tablespoon lemon juice
I¼ cups extra-virgin olive oil

½ cup fresh dill, chopped
2 cloves garlic, skinned and diced
½ teaspoon cayenne pepper
½ teaspoon salt

Add the egg and mustard to a blender bowl with I tablespoon olive oil and the lemon juice. Whirl for I minute. Then, with the blender working full speed, add ½ cup of oil to the mixture in a very thin stream, allowing the eggs to collect the fragments of oil created by the machine.

Continue until all the oil is added. Add the dill, garlic and cayenne and continue processing for another minute. Check for seasoning, add salt and pepper if necessary, then refrigerate for an hour.

RICE & VEGETABLES

BORDEN'S WILD RICE

2 cups wild rice, washed, soaked in 1 cup veal stock for
   1 hour
1 cup fresh mushrooms, cleaned and sliced
¼ pound butter

½ cup scallions and tops, chopped
1 cup diced smoked ham
1 cup burgundy wine, or more
Salt and pepper

Sauté the mushrooms in the butter until tender, then add the scallions and ham and continue cooking over low heat until the scallions have wilted thoroughly. Drain the wild rice and reserve the stock. Combine the rice, scallions, ham, the reserved cup of stock and the wine in a large pot and cover with a foil lid. Punch a silver-dollar-sized hole in the center of the foil, bring the mixture to a simmer on top of the stove and then remove to a preheated oven at 350°F for one hour, or until the moisture is absorbed. *Makes 4 cups.*

SAUTÉED MUSHROOMS

3 cups fresh mushrooms, cleaned, stemmed and sliced
1 tablespoon butter

1 tablespoon olive oil, flavored if preferred
Salt and pepper and optional additions

Olive oil raises the smoking point of butter and allows a hotter pan for this sauté. Melt butter and olive oil over moderately high heat; as soon as the foam subsides, toss in a handful of mushrooms. Toss and stir vigorously while the butter is picked up by the mushrooms. In less than 2 minutes the butter will reappear on the surface of the mushrooms. Add salt and pepper and any optional ingredients and remove. Repeat the process with another handful, being careful to keep the heat high and the number of mushrooms low. Serve immediately or reserve for later use.

Glazed Baby Onions

1 pound pearl onions, tipped and skinned
3 tablespoons olive oil

2 tablespoons red wine vinegar
Salt

Rub the onions in the olive oil and arrange in an open ovenproof dish that will allow a single layer of onions. Sprinkle the salt and vinegar over the onions and place the pan on the top rack of a preheated oven at 350°F for 30 minutes, turning the onions frequently to prevent scorching.

SEASONINGS & STOCK

PÂTÉ SALT FOR GAME BIRDS

I tablespoon freshly cracked black pepper
I tablespoon freshly cracked white pepper
I tablespoon ground nutmeg
I tablespoon ground mace
I tablespoon ground cloves

2 teaspoons mild paprika
2 teaspoons ground cayenne pepper
2 teaspoons ground marjoram
2 teaspoons thyme
2 tablespoons ground juniper berries

Grind the juniper berries in a mortar, reaching a fine powder, then blend in the other spices carefully. Salt may be added at the rate of 2 tablespoons to the foregoing. This

makes about I cup of pâté salt for game, also known as "quatre epice" when used without the juniper berry. Can be stored in an airtight jar for several months.

GAMEBIRD FUMET

2 pheasant carcasses, stripped of skin and fat
I medium carrot, sliced
I medium onion, sliced
2 tablespoons butter
2 cloves garlic, sliced

I teaspoon bouquet garni
I bay leaf
½ teaspoon thyme
2 quarts water, or half water and half red wine

Use whatever trimmed bones or carcasses you can gather, about 2 birds worth, and carefully remove all skin and fat. Using kitchen shears cut the bones in small pieces, and then in an open roasting pan brown the bones at 350°F for 15 minutes. Soften the carrot and onion in the

butter. Combine the pheasant bones with the carrot and onion, garlic, bouquet garni, bay leaf, thyme and the water and bring to a simmer. Continue simmering for 45 minutes, and remove from the heat. Strain and adjust for seasoning.

Veal Stock For Game Bird Cookery

18 pounds veal shank bones and knuckles, trimmed of
    meat, bones cut into 3-inch sections
6 cups carrots, cleaned and split
3 cups onions, peeled and sliced
18 cloves garlic, peeled and cut in half

8 bay leaves, crumbled
2 cups parsley, loosely chopped
2 teaspoons dried thyme
I pig's foot, split (optional)
10 quarts water and a large stock pot (32-quart) with lid

Separate the meat roughly from the bones to obtain a full 18 pounds of bones. Small amounts of gristle or meat and fat remaining on the bones are unimportant. Cube and reserve the meat and set aside for later use, discarding any fat. Using a heavy cleaver, split the shank bones along the vertical axis, each shank section becoming two or perhaps four pieces, and split the knuckles at least once.

In oven preheated to 400°F brown the bones in a roasting pan large enough to allow only one layer of bones. Cook for approximately 30 minutes, turning the bones periodically to avoid burning or scorching, and to allow all bones to become tinged with color. This may take several repetitions to accommodate the quantity of bones. Burned bones should be discarded.

Place the carrots, onions, garlic, parsley, and thyme in the bottom of the stock pot. As the bones become done in the oven, lay them over the vegetables until the browning of the bones is complete. Place the pot on two burners on the stove and over high heat with the cover on allow the vegetables to give off their moisture for 10 minutes.

Add I cup water and continue cooking with the lid off for 5 minutes, or until the liquid at the bottom of the pot becomes a thickened brown glaze. The bouquet should be a sure sign. Be careful not to scorch. Then repeat this procedure with a second cup of water and a few more minutes cooking, also to a glaze.

Add 10 quarts of water and the pig's foot and bring the ensemble to a boil. Skim the foam. Reduce the heat to maintain a simmer for 5 hours with the lid ajar, adding no liquids.

Brown the cubed meat in the oven without burning, and add to the stock at 5 hours and continue simmering for one additional hour, reducing the total liquid to about 5 quarts. Remove the pot from the stove. Remove all meat and bones and strain the stock. To remove all vegetables strain through a chinois and allow the stock to cool, then refrigerate overnight. The brown stock or "brun estouffade" has no salt and is ready for further reduction to make brown sauce with the addition of mushrooms, spices, Madeira and arrowroot, and sauce espagnole or demi glaze, depending on your requirements.

PASTRY

Puff Pastry

3 cups unbleached all-purpose flour
I cup cake flour
I tablespoon salt

½ teaspoon baking soda
I½ cups ice water
I pound (4 sticks) butter, frozen

Mix the flours, the salt, the soda, and the water in a chilled processor bowl. Remove the dough, form a ball, wrap in a wet towel and refrigerate.

Split each of the four sticks of butter in half length-wise with a knife and stack the pieces closely together, touching on all sides, to construct a solid square about 5 inches on a side and ¾-inch tall. Place this square between two pieces of clear plastic, and using a mallet pound the butter into a solid unit of more or less the same size. There should be no air holes or gaps. Refrigerate.

On a flour-dusted work surface, roll out the dough to a 12 x 12-inch square, turning it often and dusting with scant flour as needed to make a springy, resilient dough. Place the butter square diagonally in the center of the dough square. Turn down the corners of the dough square toward the center, just overlapping the butter.

Using a heavy rolling pin, in a direct motion to and away from yourself, roll this composite square into a rec-

tangle about 2 feet long. Don't worry about uneven ends of the dough as each turn catches these, and you begin with a square corner after each turn. Keep the pressure even on the sides, and keep the dough cold. If the butter softens, oozes or warms up, return the mixture at any time to the freezer for 30 minutes.

When the rectangle is 2 feet long, fold down the top by a third, and fold up the bottom by a third, and rotate the dough a quarter-turn to the right. The process of rolling, folding, and rotating is called a "turn." There must be a total of six turns completed for puff pastry to be expected to puff. The dough must be refrigerated at least an hour before cutting to size and baking. The pastry can be frozen, and is most easily reused when frozen flat on a baking sheet, and covered in plastic.

The pastry should be rolled out to ¼-inch thickness and baked at 450°F for 10 minutes on the lower rack of the oven, then covered and cooked 400°F for an additional 30 minutes.

PÂTÉ BRISÉE

5 cups flour
2 teaspoons salt
1 pound butter, cut in small bits

4 eggs, lightly beaten
¼ cup cold water

Mound the flour in a mixing bowl, and form a well to receive the salt and butter. Using your fingers blend the flour and salt and butter until you have a crumbly dough.

Add the egg and water and continue kneading until the dough forms a ball. Do not overwork. Wrap the ball in plastic and refrigerate for at least 1 hour. This dough will hold for 12 hours, refrigerated.

(*Makes about 3½ pounds of pastry*)

SUPPLIERS

American Institute of Wine & Food
1550 Bryant Street, Suite # 700
San Francisco, California 94103-4832
(415) 255-3000

Bridge Kitchenware
214 52nd Street
New York, New York 10022
(212) 838-1901

Czimer's Game and Sea Foods, Inc.
13136 W. 159th Street
Lockport, Illinois 60441-8767
(708) 301-0500

D'Artagnan, Inc., Game Suppliers
280 Wilson Avenue
Newark, New Jersey 07105
(973) 344-0565

Fare Game Food Company
P.O. Box 18431
Rochester, New York 14618
(716) 473-4210

Manchester Quail Farms
P.O. Box 97
3525 Camden Highway
Dalzell, South Carolina 29040
(800) 845-0421

Matfer Kitchen and Bakery Equipment Co.
16249 Stagg Street
Van Nuys, California 91406
(818) 782-0792

Morris Lobel & Sons, Inc., "Butchers to the Stars"
1096 Madison Avenue
New York, New York 10028
(800) 5-L-O-B-E-L-S. Or (212) 737-1372

POLARICA (game, poultry, berries)
105 Quint Street
San Francisco, California 94124
1-800-Game-USA

Williams-Sonoma Inc.
P.O. Box 7456
San Francisco, California 94120-7456
(800) 541-2233

INDEX